BRAIN GAMES

MW00889849

ENGINEERING
SCIENCE
EXPERIMENTS

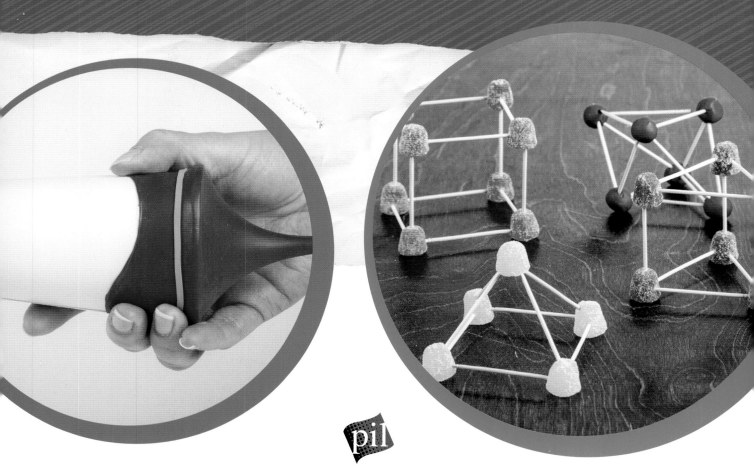

pil

Publications International, Ltd.

Written by Nicole Sulgit and Beth Taylor with additional material by Adam Parrilli
Photo styling by Nick LaShure, Ashley Joyce, and Nicole Sulgit
Photography by Christopher Hiltz, Nick LaShure and Nicole Sulgit
Additional images from Shutterstock.com

ISBN: 978-1-64558-524-4

Manufactured in China.

8 7 6 5 4 3 2 1

SAFETY WARNING
All of the experiments and activities in this book MUST be performed with adult supervision. All projects contain a degree of risk, so carefully read all instructions before you begin and make sure that you have safety materials such as goggles, gloves, etc. Also make sure that you have safety equipment, such as a fire extinguisher and first aid kit, on hand. You are assuming the risk of any injury by conducting these activities and experiments. Publications International, Ltd. will not be liable for any injury or property damage.

Let's get social!
@Publications_International
@PublicationsInternational
@BrainGames.TM
www.pilbooks.com

CONTENTS

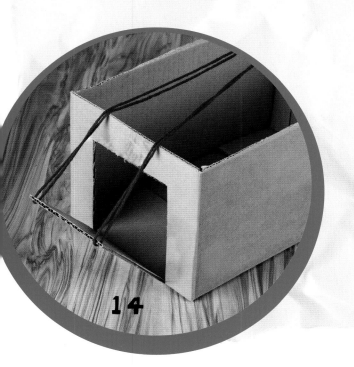

INTRODUCTION

STEM stands for science, technology, engineering, and math. In *Engineering Science Experiments,* you'll be engineering as you build and test, but you'll also be exploring scientific principles, using math, and using and building different technologies.

While we include step-by-step instructions for each experiment, you may find a different way to do things. If an experiment leaves you with questions, you can create your own experiments and try to answer them.

Engineers follow a certain set of steps as they work, called the Engineering Design Process. There are usually 5 to 7 steps that include identifying a problem that needs solving, researching it, brainstorming and planning a solution, testing that solution, and refining the plan based on the results. One simple 5-step Engineering Design Process uses these words: Ask, Imagine, Plan, Create, Improve.

ASK

What is the problem? What do you know about the problem? Have other people tried to solve the problem? What materials do you have available to solve the problem?

IMAGINE

How might you solve the problem? How many ideas can you come up with? As you work, you might find yourself asking more questions, too!

PLAN

Of your potential solutions, which seems best? What materials do you need? What do you expect the finished product to look like? Engineers often produce sketches or diagrams.

CREATE

Engineers don't move straight from a diagram to a finished product. Instead, they create a model called a prototype. They see how it works—or doesn't work!

IMPROVE

You can learn from problems as well as successes! From problems, you can learn how to improve the prototype. Sometimes, you'll go back to the drawing board and brainstorm a new solution.

MEASUREMENTS

There have been many systems of measurement used throughout history. In ancient times, people needed ways to trade goods, to build houses and navigate on boats, and to record rainfall and the levels of rivers and streams.

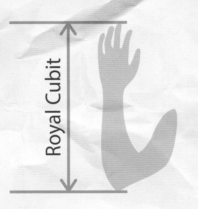

Royal Cubit

ANCIENT SYSTEMS OF MEASUREMENT

A number of ancient civilizations used a measurement called the cubit. A cubit in ancient Egypt wasn't the same length as a cubit in ancient Greece or ancient Rome, though. The length of a cubit varied from culture to culture and over time, although it often corresponded roughly to the approximate length of a person's elbow to the tip of their middle finger.

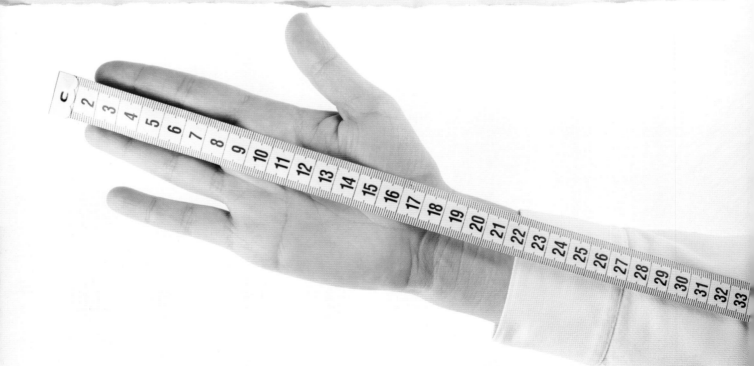

Diamonds don't grow on trees! But the word carat, used to measure the mass of a diamond or other gemstones, comes from the word "carob." The seeds of the carob tree were used as a way to measure mass, including the mass of gemstones.

MODERN SYSTEMS OF MEASUREMENT

The International System of Units is also called the metric system. It defines seven "base units" and then measures everything in comparison to them. For example, a meter is used to define length. A meter is the distance traveled by light in a vacuum during a time interval of 1/299792458 of a second.

K	kelvin temperature
m	meter (distance)
A	ampere (electric current)
s	second (time)
mol	mole (amount of substance)
kg	kilogram (mass)
cd	candela (intensity of light)

While the metric system is used by scientists in the United States, in daily life a system based on an older British system is used. Miles, feet, and inches are all part of that system. A foot is twelve inches. How does that compare to the length of your foot? What about an adult's foot?

BUILD YOUR OWN SCALE

You can create your own scale to determine whether one object is lighter or heavier than another.

MATERIALS

- Yarn
- Scissors
- Two paper cups
- Hanger
- Ruler
- Small objects such as beans or seeds

Step 1

Measure and cut two equal lengths of yarn. A foot is a good length.

Step 2

Carefully poke two holes in each cup.

Step 3

Thread one piece of yarn through each cup.

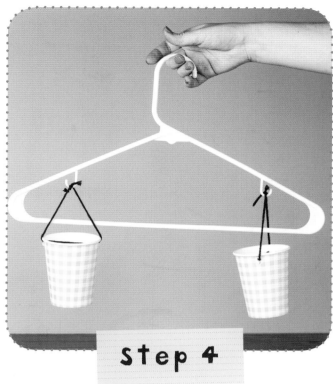

Step 4

Tie the cups to each side of the hanger.

Step 5

Pour the beans or seeds into one cup.

Step 6

The hanger will tilt downward. You can balance it again by putting beans in the other cup.

MACHINES AND TOOLS

What pops into your head when you hear the word "machine"? Maybe you think of a washing machine, a robot, or a furnace—something complex, with many mechanical parts. But some machines are very simple. They're so basic you may not think of them as machines at all!

SIX SIMPLE MACHINES

The six "simple machines" are the inclined plane, the wedge, the lever, the wheel and axle, the pulley, and the screw. Each of these machines helps humans do work. To scientists, "work" doesn't mean something like doing your homework. Work is done when someone—or something—applies a force that moves an object over a distance. When you throw a ball, you are doing work. Simple machines make it easier for you to do work.

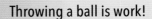

Throwing a ball is work!

When you go up a ramp, you are using a machine—an **inclined plane**. It's easier to push an object up a ramp than it is to lift it straight up.

When you apply a force to one end of the **wedge**, it transports that force to the sharp edge of the wedge.

Have you played on a seesaw? Then you've used a **lever**! A lever has two parts: one long part such as a beam rests on a support, called a fulcrum. You apply force to one side of the lever to move it. In the picture, a painter uses a screwdriver as a lever to open the paint can. The edge of the paint can acts as a fulcrum. In the last experiment, the scale was a lever that balanced on a central fulcrum.

A steering wheel is an example of a **wheel and axle**. Connect a cylinder, or rod, to a wheel to form this simple machine.

A **pulley** helps you change the direction of a force. With a simple pulley, you pull down to make something go up!

The edges on **screws** are called threads.

RAMP

You can create an inclined plane with simple household objects.

MATERIALS

- Books
- Sturdy cardboard (we used the cardboard from the back of a legal pad)
- Toy car or truck

Step 1

Set up a shallow ramp.

Step 2

Hold the toy car at the top of the ramp.

Step 3

Let it go. How fast and how far does it go?

Step 4

Make your ramp steeper. How does this affect the car's speed and distance?

Step 5

Make your ramp even steeper. How does this affect the car's speed and distance?

Step 6

At what point is the ramp so steep that the car cannot make it safely down the ramp?

On mountains, roads need to be built so that cars can make it up and down safely. You'll see a switchback formation rather than a straight, steep road.

DRAWBRIDGE

Create a simple pulley system to raise
and lower your castle drawbridge.

MATERIALS

- Box
- Yarn
- Ruler
- Scissors
- Marker or pen
- Toy soldiers or prin-
  cesses. animal figures.
  or toy cars (optional)

Step 1

Cut any flaps or lids
off the box.

Step 2

Using the ruler and pen or marker, outline a rectangular shape on the box.

Step 3

Ask an adult for help with this step! Cut a flap in the box. Use the tips of the scissors or a hole punch to make two small holes, one on the top left corner of the flap and the other on the top right.

Step 4

Measure two lengths of string or yarn, each about 36 inches (91 cm) long.

Step 5

Thread the yarn through the holes in the flaps.

Step 6

You can now raise and lower your drawbridge, letting in–or keeping out–soldiers, cars, or other figures!

CASTLE DEFENSES

A drawbridge was one way to control the entry of people into a castle. Castles were built in medieval times for specific purposes and their architecture was tailored for those purposes.

What's the difference between a castle and a palace?

Both are places where members of the nobility—dukes, earls, and so forth—or royalty live. But palaces are not fortified. Castles are not only residences but fortresses, meant to defend and protect.

Buckingham Palace

Towers were a common feature of castles. They allowed for a view of the surrounding countryside. One tower called the keep was the last place of refuge during a war. People retreated to this last line of defense.

Defensive walls surrounded the complex. Castle defenders could launch a counterattack from the walkways. Concentric castles had multiple walls nested inside each other.

Narrow vertical openings allowed for the release of arrows.

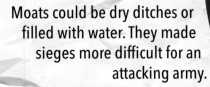

Moats could be dry ditches or filled with water. They made sieges more difficult for an attacking army.

COIN SORTER

Sort objects based on size with this easy machine that uses gravity to do its work.

MATERIALS

- Empty tissue box
- Cardboard tube
- Sturdy tape
- Scissors
- Ruler or measuring tape
- Pen or pencil
- Coins

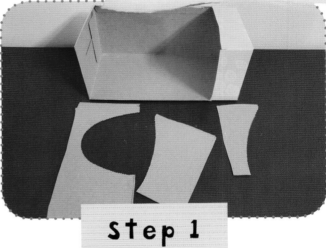

Step 1

Cut off the top and front panels of the tissue box, leaving a bit of a ledge on one side for the chute to rest against.

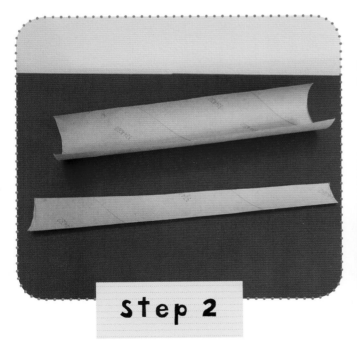

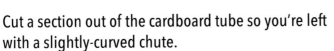

Step 2

Cut a section out of the cardboard tube so you're left with a slightly-curved chute.

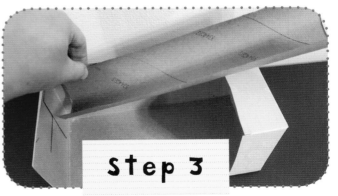

Step 3

Hold the chute against the tissue box to get an idea of where you will cut the three holes in steps 4 and 5. The largest coins, the quarters, will fall off the end of the chute.

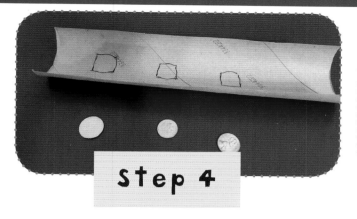

Step 4

Draw a square outline around each coin. You will need to be precise, as coins are very similar in size. Use a ruler or measuring tape to make sure the holes are accurate and in a row.

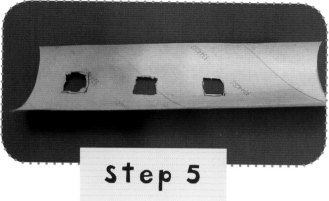

Step 5

Cut out the outlines for each coin. It is probably easiest to score the cardboard with one end of the scissors and then carefully punch out the hole. Ask an adult for help with this step.

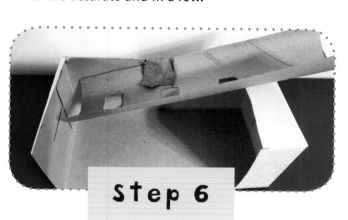

Step 6

Tape the chute in place. Remember to leave a little space at the end for the quarter to fall through. The hole for the smallest coin is at the top of the chute.

Step 7

Using the leftover cardboard from step 1, tape panels between the holes to the bottom of the box to create compartments that separate the coins.

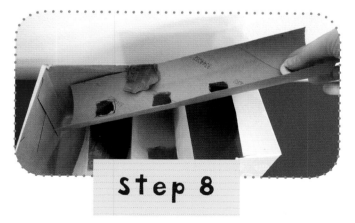

Step 8

Hold a coin at the top and let it slide down the chute! The smaller coins will fall through the smaller holes at the top of the chute, while the larger ones will skate on by.

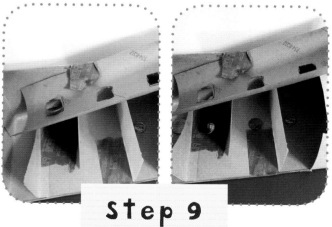

Step 9

If your coin sorter isn't working, you may need to widen the holes or narrow them by adding a piece of tape to one side.

MONEY MATTERS

The coin sorter you made sorted coins based on one attribute, their size. And the tools you had available made accuracy a challenge. Pennies and dimes are almost identical in size. So how do vending machines and other machines quickly detect differences in coin denominations?

You may have seen coin-counting machines at stores that allow you to bring in pennies in order to exchange them for cash, gift cards, or store credit. Inside, these machines have automated sensors that allow them to detect the size and thickness of different kinds of coins. Those sensors can determine size more accurately and with a greater degree of precision than our homemade model.

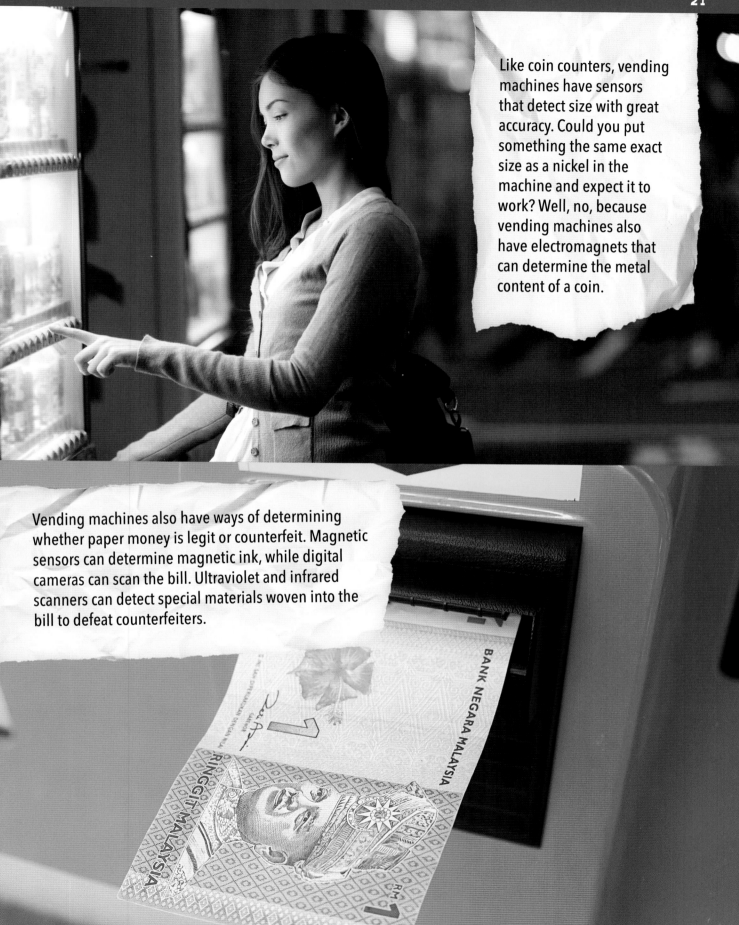

Like coin counters, vending machines have sensors that detect size with great accuracy. Could you put something the same exact size as a nickel in the machine and expect it to work? Well, no, because vending machines also have electromagnets that can determine the metal content of a coin.

Vending machines also have ways of determining whether paper money is legit or counterfeit. Magnetic sensors can determine magnetic ink, while digital cameras can scan the bill. Ultraviolet and infrared scanners can detect special materials woven into the bill to defeat counterfeiters.

WHEELBARROW

Pushing a load makes it easier to move than carrying it. Try it out with a wheelbarrow.

MATERIALS

- Cardboard box
- 2 long or 4 short pieces of wood
- Short pencil
- Spool
- Tape
- Scissors

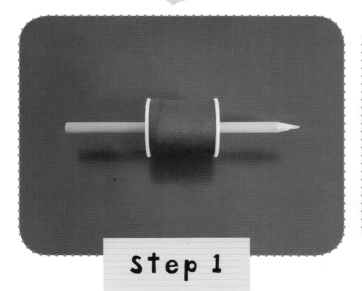

Step 1

The spool will be the wheel of your wheelbarrow. Thread the pencil through the hole.

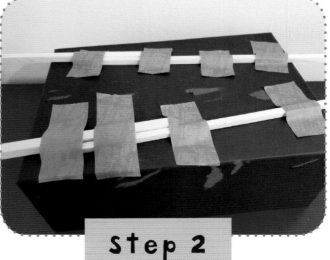

Step 2

Tape the wooden strips to the box.

Step 3

Secure the ends of the wooden strips to the ends of the pencil with tape.

Step 4

Use your wheelbarrow!

Wheels are a type of lever. You apply the force to the handles, and the wheel acts as the fulcrum to move the load.

SHAPES AND STRUCTURES

Geometry, a branch of mathematics, helps you learn about shapes—not just squares and circles, but three-dimensional shapes like cones, cylinders, and spheres. People use geometry when they're trying to figure out how much can fit in a box, or how much paint to buy to paint a room in their house.

HOW MANY SIDES?

Most buildings have four sides, but the Pentagon is in the shape of a five-sided pentagon. Originally, it was going to be built in a different location, on a piece of land with roughly five sides, so the design matched the space. Even when a different location was chosen, the five-sided design was still used.

Euclid, who lived in ancient Greece, is considered the father of geometry. He wrote a book about math called *Elements* that was used for centuries.

Shapes can be used in art and design. This type of pattern is called a tessellation.

TOOTHPICK S.T.E.M. STRUCTURES

MATERIALS

- Toothpicks
- Gumdrops
- Observation notebook

Build 3-D shapes using toothpicks and gumdrops, mini marshmallows, or balls of modeling clay. Then record the number of faces, edges, and vertices of each shape in an observation notebook. Faces are the shape's surfaces. Edges are the line segments where two faces meet. Vertices are the points or corners where edges meet.

CUBE

Step 1

Form a square for the base with 4 toothpicks and a gumdrop in each of the 4 corners. You can also use mini marshmallows or balls of modeling clay.

Step 2

Stick another toothpick into the top of each gumdrop. The new toothpicks should stand upright on top of the square base.

Step 3

Create another square as you did in step 1. Position the second square on top of the vertical toothpicks and connect to complete the cube. *How many faces, edges, and vertices does the cube have?* Record results in your observation notebook.

SQUARE PYRAMID

A pyramid is a solid shape that rises to a single point. All of the faces (sides) that are not the base must be triangles.

Step 1

Form a square for the base with 4 toothpicks and 4 gumdrops.

Step 2

Stick a toothpick into each gumdrop of the base at an angle so that the ends meet in the center.

Step 3

Connect the unattached ends of the toothpicks to another gumdrop to complete the square pyramid. *How many faces, edges, and vertices does the square pyramid have?* Record results in your observation notebook.

TRIANGULAR PRISM

A prism has the same top and bottom shape,
connected by rectangles or parallelograms.

Step 1

Form a triangle for the base with
3 toothpicks and 3 gumdrops.

Step 2

Stick another toothpick into the top of each
gumdrop. The new toothpicks should stand upright
on top of the square base.

Step 3

Make another triangle as you did in
step 1. Position the second triangle on
top of the vertical toothpicks and connect
to complete the triangular prism. *How
many faces, edges, and vertices does the
triangular prism have?* Record results in
your observation notebook.

TIP:

Your S.T.E.M. structures will be strongest if you stick the toothpicks into the gumdrops at the correct
angle and don't reposition them. Forming a 2-D shape with toothpicks alone (and no gumdrops) first
helps you see the correct angles. Once you've inserted a toothpick at the angle you want, push the
toothpick almost all the way through the gumdrop.

STANDING ON EGGS

Will eggs break if you stand on them? Try it and see!
(Wash your feet before and after doing this.)

MATERIALS

- 1 or 2 cartons of raw eggs

Step 1

Open the cartons and place them side-by-side. Take off your shoes so you are barefoot.

Step 2
Have someone help you step up on the eggs.

Step 3
Do they break?
Why not?

WHY DOES IT WORK?

Why can the eggs withstand the force of your feet? Part of it is that your weight is evenly distributed. Weight focused on a specific part of the egg can crack the shell. When you crack an egg to break it while baking, you focus a force at one point.

Try this with an adult's permission. Rest an egg on a countertop, on top of a paper towel. Press the palm of your hand downward on the egg, trying to break it. Have the grown up try too. It's difficult! But when you tap the egg gently against a sharp edge, it will crack. (Always wash your hands after handling raw eggs.)

Part of the answer has to do with the shape of the egg. Eggs are arches, which are strong shapes that can support a lot of weight. They are a common bridge shape for that reason.

Have you ever seen shoes advertise good arch support? The majority of people have feet that have a natural arch shape that helps support weight! (Not everyone does.)

PAPER TOWER

How high can you build a tower made only from paper and tape?

MATERIALS

- Printer paper
- Masking or clear tape

Step 1

Make a cylindrical roll from a piece of paper. Make sure the ends are lined up neatly.

Step 2

Tape the paper into place.

Step 3

Make two more rolls to form the base of the tower.

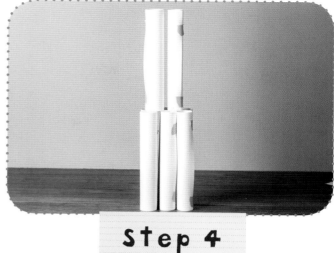

Step 4

Now comes the hard part–form a new row by balancing two more rolls of paper on top.

Step 5

Now comes the trickiest part of all. Can you add one more roll to the very top?

FOR AN EXTRA CHALLENGE

In our first example, we rolled each paper along the short side. Let's try rolling along the long side this time. Adding a flat piece of paper between rows may help.

FURTHER EXPERIMENTATION

Vary the size of the cylindrical rolls to see if it helps you make the structure more or less sound. Try this experiment on different surfaces to see if one works better than others. If you use more than three cylindrical rolls for the bottom base, how high can your tower go?

HOUSE OF CARDS

With care, precision, and a little bit of luck, you can build a very high structure from flimsy paper cards.

MATERIALS

- A deck of cards, preferably an older one
- A flat surface. Surfaces with texture will work better than smooth ones.

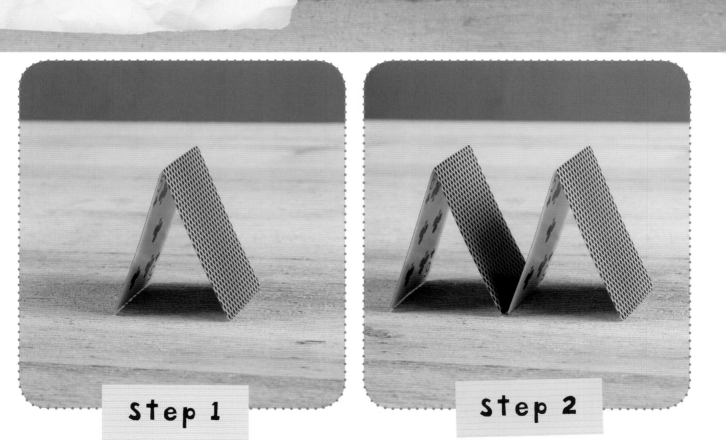

Step 1

Prop two cards against each other.

Step 2

Prop two more cards against each other.

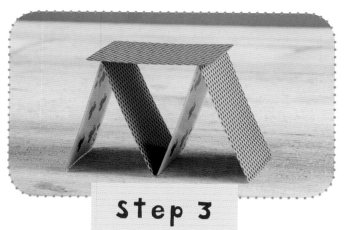

step 3

Balance a card on top of your two triangular pyramids.

step 4

Balance two more cards in a pyramid above it.

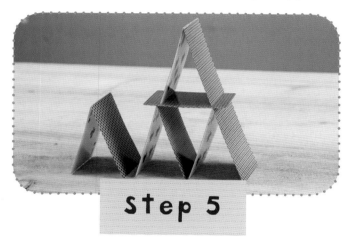

step 5

You can expand your house by building to the left or right.

step 6

With a wider base, you can build your house higher as well.

This is the basic structure of your house of cards. See how tall you can build your house!

DID YOU KNOW?

In 2007, a man named Bryan Berg set the Guiness World Record for the tallest house of cards. It was more than 25 feet (7.8 meters) tall!

IN THE
WATER

We spend most of our lives on land, but about 70 percent of Earth's surface is covered by water. Water and other liquids can exhibit fascinating, unexpected behavior. There is even a branch of physics called fluid mechanics that examines how liquids, gases, and plasmas work.

BUOYANCY

Some objects float and some objects sink. The force of gravity works to push an object downward. The force of buoyancy pushes an object upward. If an object is more dense than the liquid, it will sink. Objects that are less dense will float. That does not depend on the size of the object or how heavy it is. While we might expect that big objects will sink and smaller objects will float, that is not true. Otherwise a coin would float when you toss it in a fountain, and large ships would sink.

Buoys–floating objects that act as markers– are buoyant!

ARCHIMEDES'S PRINCIPLE

When you put something in water, it displaces the water—that is, it moves it. Thousands of years ago, a man named Archimedes of Syracuse described a law of physics. He said that an object is buoyed up by a force equal to the weight of the water it displaces. If the force is strong enough—if enough water is displaced—the object floats.

Scuba divers use something called a buoyancy control device (BCD) to help them stay at the depth they want to stay at.

WALKING WATER

Do you think you can get water to defy gravity and walk from one glass to another? Try this experiment to find out!

MATERIALS

- 5 clear glasses
- Food coloring in 3 colors
- 4 half-sheet paper towels
- Spoon
- Water
- Scissors

Step 1

Line up 5 clear glasses in a row. We are using 9-ounce plastic glasses. Fill the first, third, and fifth glasses about ¾ full with water.

Step 2

Add a few drops of food coloring to each water-filled glass, using a different color for each. Stir with a spoon until well blended. Clean the spoon after each glass to prevent color transfers.

Step 3

Fold each half-sheet paper towel like an accordion into a strip about 1 inch wide.

Step 4

Fold each strip in half to form a V shape. The V should be a little taller than the glasses. Trim any excess off the paper towel ends.

Step 5

Flip the V shape upside down. Place one end in a glass with colored water and the other end in an adjacent empty glass.

Step 6

Repeat with the other glasses in the row, placing a paper towel strip between each pair of adjacent glasses.

Step 7

Take a break! This experiment moves very slowly, so you can check back later. *What do you observe after 30 minutes? What do you observe the next day?*

HOW DOES IT WORK?

The water moves up the paper towels (seeming to defy gravity) through a process called capillary action. Water gets pulled into the tiny gaps between the fibers of the paper towels and eventually down into the empty glasses. The gaps in the paper towel act like capillary tubes and pull the water upward. This process is what helps water travel up from the roots of a plant to the rest of the plant.

SOAP BOAT

Can you move a paper boat forward using nothing but soap?

MATERIALS

- Cardstock
- Scissors
- Toothpick
- Dishwashing liquid
- Shallow tray or container of water

Step 1

Cut out a boat shape from the cardstock. The front of the boat has a point like the roof of a house, and the back of the boat has a notch cut out.

Step 2

Fill a shallow tray or container with water. Place your boat on the surface at one end and point it forward. Act quickly before the paper boat starts to curl! Dip a toothpick in dishwashing liquid.

Step 3

Drop a single drop of dishwashing liquid onto the water in the notch in the back of the boat. *What happens?*

HOW DOES IT WORK?

The paper boat moves due to a force called surface tension. Water molecules are strongly attracted and cling close together, especially on the surface. This attraction creates surface tension. Adding soap to the water weakens the bonds behind the boat, reducing surface tension. As a result, the rest of the water surface pulls away, dragging the boat along with it.

These bugs, called water striders, stay on top of water because of surface tension. Their long, thin legs keep their weight balanced as they move lightly across the water.

When you see a water droplet on a leaf, it's an example of surface tension. The water is pulled into a loose sphere.

LOAD A BOAT

Aluminum foil seems like it would make a flimsy boat—but it can carry more than you think!

MATERIALS

- Bowl of water
- Aluminum foil
- Pennies or other small objects that act as "cargo" for your boat

Step 1

Tear off a sheet of aluminum foil for your boat.

Step 2

Step 3

Fold it in half. Turn it up at the edges to make a small square with raised edges.

Place your boat in the water.

Step 4

Begin loading the cargo in your boat.

CAN YOU GET YOUR BOAT TO SINK?

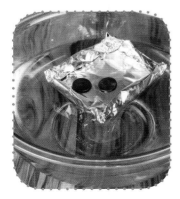

NOW, EXPERIMENT!

Will a larger, wider boat carry more?
What if you use a double sheet of foil?

BOATS

Boats and rafts have been used since prehistoric times for trade and travel to new places. The islands of Oceania and Australia were first settled between 40,000 and 60,000 years ago by sea travel.

Dugout canoes are carved out from logs. Canoes that date back 8,000 years have been found in Africa and Asia.

Some boats rely on humans to power them with oars or poles. Kayaks were first used by indigenous people such as the Aleut and Inuit.

Triremes were used in war by ancient Mediterranean civilizations. While they had sails, they relied heavily on oar power.

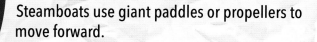

Steamboats use giant paddles or propellers to move forward.

Many sailboats have small motors or diesel engines to help sailors get in and out of harbors or for backup.

SODA CAN SUBMARINE

Submarines control how they rise and fall through the use of air. See how it works in this experiment.

MATERIALS

- Empty soda can
- Short length of tubing
- Container full of water, deeper than the soda can

Step 1

Fill the soda can with water and insert the tube into the can.

Step 2

Submerge the submarine. If it rises to the surface, add more water into the soda can so it is completely full and sinks. Leave the other end of the tubing above the water.

Step 3

Blow into the tube. As air travels along the tube and fills the can, the can rises again.

SUBMARINES

Submarines have been around for a long time. In fact, an inventor named David Bushnell invented a kind of submarine that was used during the American Revolutionary War! He called it the *Turtle*. Submarines today look a lot different. Modern submarines are powered by engines or nuclear power.

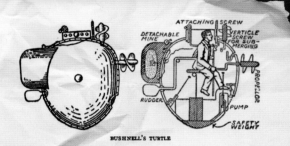

BUSHNELL'S TURTLE

Submarines can hold a lot of people. On a nuclear-powered submarine used by the military, the crew can consist of more than 100 people.

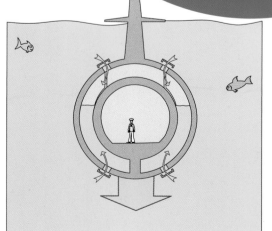

Submarines have tanks of water called ballast. Water weighs the submarine down as it submerges. Water is released from the tank when it is ready to rise. Propellers move the submarine forward.

Submarines can be used for scientific exploration and to explore shipwrecks. This submarine, found at a museum in Monaco, was used by Jacques Cousteau, a famous oceanographer.

Submarines navigate through sonar equipment.

Periscopes were developed so submarines could search the surface for targets or threats without surfacing completely.

IN THE AIR

Orville and Wilbur Wright took their first successful flight at Kitty Hawk in 1903. Since then, planes have grown larger and faster. But planes weren't the first airborne objects. People had been using hang gliders and balloons long before the Wright Brothers were born. How have humans managed to keep objects in the air? They have come to an understanding of four forces that affect airplane flight: weight, lift, thrust, and drag.

WEIGHT

If you jump in the air, you will return to the Earth. That's the force of gravity, or weight, acting on you. Weight acts on airplanes, balloons, and kites too.

LIFT

Lift pushes an object upward, countering its weight. The wings of an airplane are instrumental in keeping it aloft. They are shaped so that the air pressure underneath the wing is higher than the pressure above the wing, which helps keep the airplane up. If you are on an airplane, you may see flaps extend or retract during the flight, especially during takeoff or landing. Changes in the shape of the wing help control the airplane.

THRUST

Thrust is the force that sets the airplane in motion and keeps it moving in the right direction. In airplanes, engines produce thrust. When you throw a paper airplane, you are providing thrust.

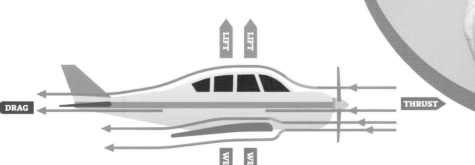

DRAG

Just as weight and lift are opposite forces, thrust and drag are opposite forces. Drag works to slow an aircraft down.

AIR VORTEX CANNON

Create an air vortex cannon—a simple device that shoots out bursts of air. Then test how far you can shoot air from your cannon.

MATERIALS

- Paper or plastic cup
- Rubber band
- Balloon
- Scissors
- Craft knife
- Tape
- Toilet paper
- Measuring tape

Step 1

With an adult's help, use a craft knife or scissors to cut a circular hole in the bottom of the cup. We are using a 9-ounce paper cup.

Step 2

Inflate the balloon to stretch it out, then deflate it. Tie a knot in the neck of the deflated balloon.

Step 3

Use scissors to cut off the top of the balloon, on the opposite side as the tied neck.

Step 4

Step 5

Stretch the balloon over the top of the cup, with the tied neck facing outward and the excess balloon overlapping on all sides.

Wrap a rubber band around the top of the cup to secure the balloon beneath the lip of the cup.

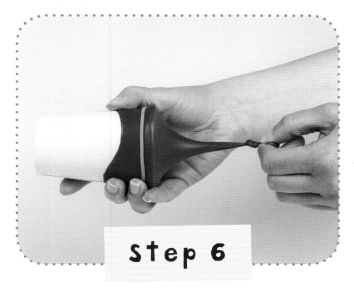

Step 6

Step 7

To fire your air vortex cannon, pinch the tied knot of the stretched balloon, pull back gently, and release. Now you are ready to test how far air from your cannon can shoot.

Tape a strip of toilet paper to a doorframe. Stand directly in front of the toilet paper and fire your cannon. Step back and fire again. Find the maximum distance from which air shooting from your cannon can travel while still exerting enough force to move the toilet paper. Measure and record the distance.

HOW DOES IT WORK?

Your air vortex cannon works by quickly applying force to air molecules inside the cup. When the balloon surface snaps forward, it collides directly with the air molecules inside the cup, forcing them out of the hole. When this fast-moving air shoots out of the cannon and mixes with the stationary air outside, it forms a vortex ring.

PAPER AIRPLANES

Investigate aerodynamics–the interaction between air and the objects moving through the air. Create and test three different paper airplane models. Which plane will fly farthest? Which will fly fastest? Which will fly straightest?

THE NEEDLE

This classic plane is built for speed–the harder you chuck it, the farther it goes.

Step 1

Using a ruler, draw the lines you see on a blank sheet of paper. Fold the paper in half on the center line, and open up the paper so it lies flat.

Step 2

Fold down both corners.

Step 3

Fold down the sides.

Step 4

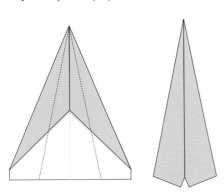

Fold down the sides once more.

Step 5

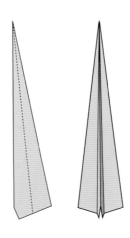

Fold the plane in half along the center line. Then fold down each wing.

CLOUD DRAGON

This unusual design has a stabilizing forewing known as a canard.

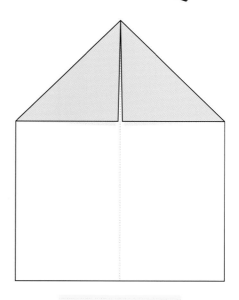

Step 1

Begin with a blank sheet of paper. Fold paper in half on center line, and open up paper so that it lies flat.

Step 2

Fold down both top corners.

Step 3

Turn plane over. Fold down both sides.

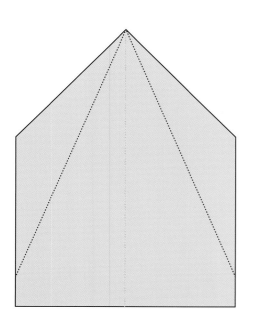

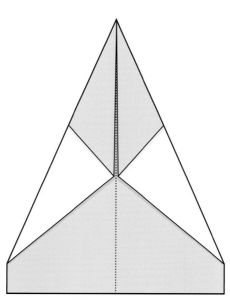

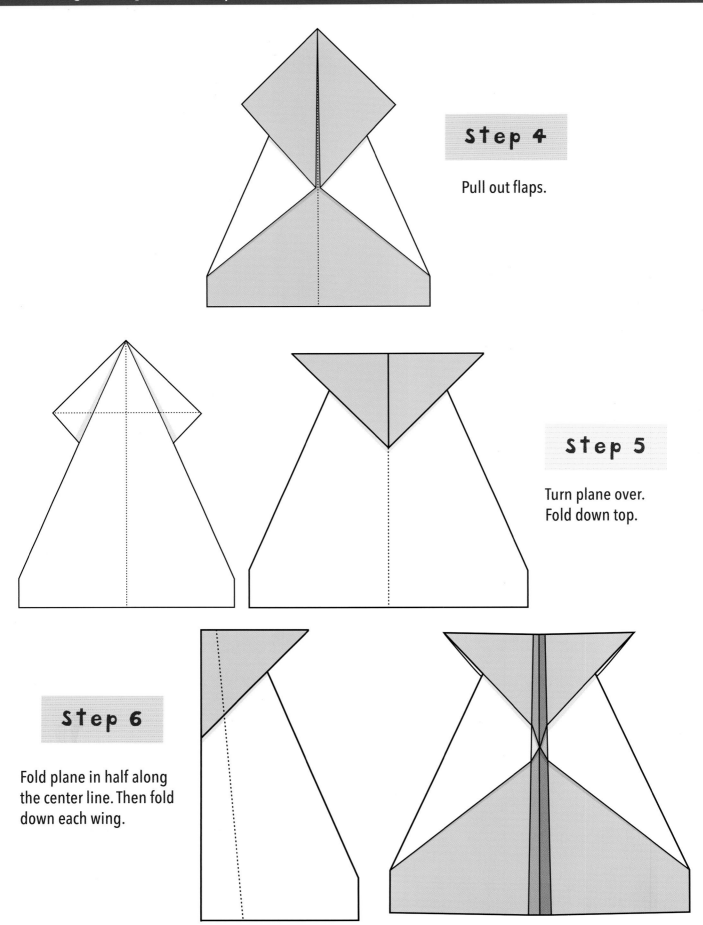

Step 4

Pull out flaps.

Step 5

Turn plane over.
Fold down top.

Step 6

Fold plane in half along
the center line. Then fold
down each wing.

BLUE YONDER

Blue Yonder is a glider that lives up to its name. With a good launch, this far-flying craft will go sailing into the blue!

Step 1

Begin with a blank piece of paper. Fold paper in half (from left to right).

Step 2

Fold back each top corner.

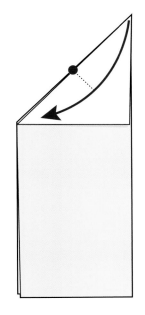

Step 3

Fold the top point down to create a crease.

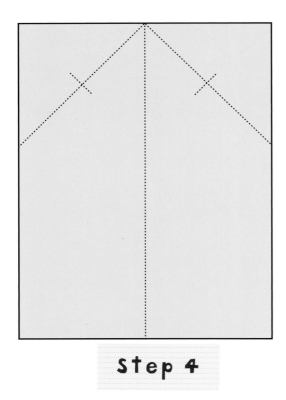

Step 4

Unfold paper and lay it flat.

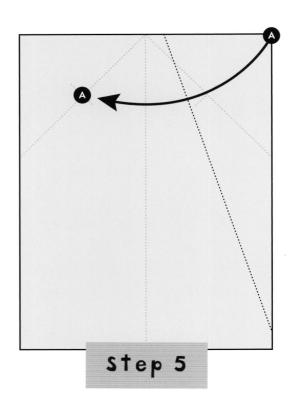

Step 5

Fold top corner to meet point A.

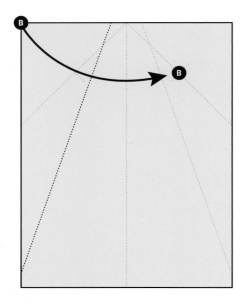

Step 6

Unfold. Repeat on the other side.

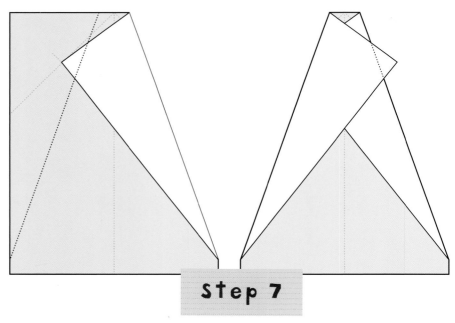

Step 7

Fold the two sides along the creases you just made. Fold and tuck the two points inward.

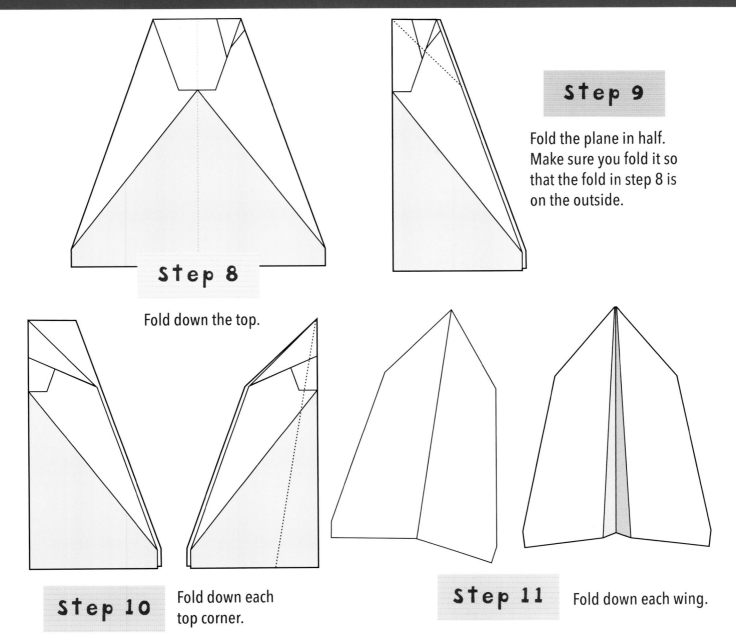

Step 8

Fold down the top.

Step 9

Fold the plane in half. Make sure you fold it so that the fold in step 8 is on the outside.

Step 10

Fold down each top corner.

Step 11

Fold down each wing.

NOW TRY THIS!

Fly all your planes. Which model stays in the air longest? Which model is fastest? The Needle speeds through the air because air passes around its streamlined shape easily without exerting much drag. Blue Yonder experiences lots of lift because its wings have a large area, allowing it to stay aloft longer.

PAPER ROCKETS

Make two paper rockets—one with fins and one without—and test which is more stable.

MATERIALS

- Cardstock paper
- Two plastic straws
- Scissors
- Pencil
- Tape

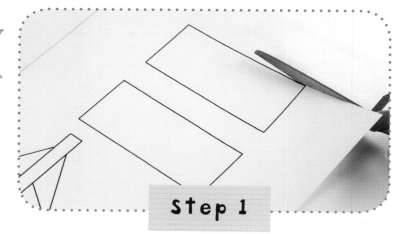

Step 1

Carefully cut out a 2" x 4 ½" rectangle. This will form the body tube of your rocket. Color or decorate, if desired.

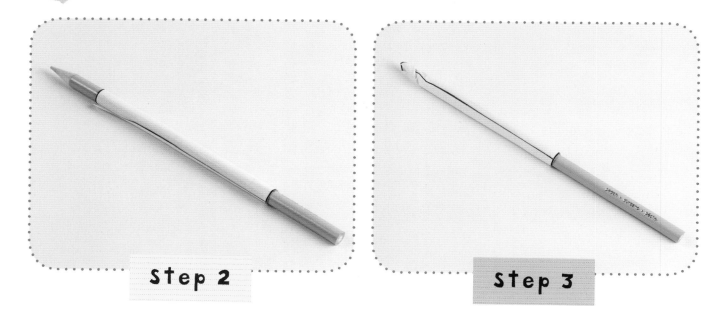

Step 2

Wrap the rectangle lengthwise around a pencil. Tape paper closed so that it forms a tube, but don't use tape at the very top end of the tube near the pencil tip.

Step 3

Twist the top of the body tube around the sharpened pencil tip, being careful not to rip the paper. This is the nose cone. Slide the rocket off the pencil. This completes the rocket without fins.

Step 4

Make another rocket following steps 1–3. This time you will add fins. Draw and cut out 2 fin units like the ones you see above.

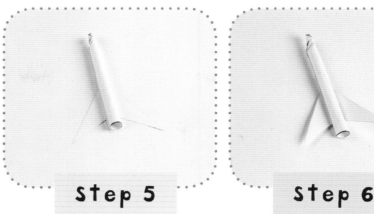

Step 5

Each fin unit has 2 triangular fins separated by a narrow rectangle. Lay the first fin unit flat with outlines facing down. Place the body tube on top of the rectangle so the bottom of the rectangle aligns with the bottom of the body tube.

Step 6

Cut a piece of tape in half so you have 2 narrow pieces. Tape the fin unit to the body tube using one piece to wrap around the bottom of the rectangle and the other to wrap around the top of the rectangle.

Step 7

Repeat steps 5–6 for the other fin unit, but tape it on the other side of the body tube. Both fin units should now be on opposite sides of the bottom of the rocket.

Step 8

Fold the fins up along the parallel lines on either side of the rectangle. The 4 fins should form a "+" shape, with each fin at a right angle (90 degrees) from its neighbor. This completes the rocket with fins.

Step 9

Compare the rockets. Slide each onto a straw and blow to launch. *Which rocket flies farther? Do the rockets fly straight or tumble in midair? Do fins make a rocket more stable?*

HOW DOES IT WORK?

The fins on your second rocket help keep it stable and pointed in the same direction. The rocket with fins should have flown straight and traveled farther as a result.

CRAFT STICK
CATAPULT

Catapults are simple machines that have been used since ancient times to hurl projectiles at enemies. Make your own catapult out of craft sticks and then test how far you can launch projectiles.

MATERIALS

- 8 jumbo craft sticks
- 5 rubber bands
- Bottle lid or cap
- Glue
- Pompoms or other soft projectiles
- Measuring tape or ruler

Step 1

Stack 6 jumbo craft sticks on top of each other. Secure the sticks together by tightly wrapping a rubber band around each end of the stack.

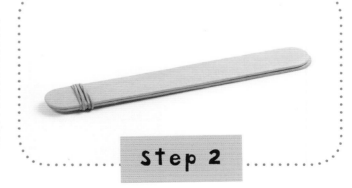

Step 2

Next, stack 2 craft sticks on top of each other. Secure tightly with a rubber band around just one end.

step 3

Slide the stack of 6 sticks in between the unsecured end of the 2 sticks from step 2 as far as possible.

step 4

Use 2 more rubber bands to secure both parts in place so that the rubber bands form an "X" where all the sticks meet.

step 5

Add a dab of glue to the end of the launching arm that sticks up. Press the bottle lid down onto the glue. Hold firmly until glue is dry.

step 6

To launch a projectile, place a pompom or other small object in the bottle lid. Hold the base of the catapult down with one hand. With the other hand, push the launching arm down and release! *How far can you launch your projectile? Measure with a ruler or measuring tape. What happens when you push the launching arm farther down?*

HOW DOES IT WORK?

Catapults work because energy can be converted from one type to another and transferred from one object to another. When you push down the launching arm, you add energy to it. This energy is stored as potential energy until you're ready to launch. When you let go, this stored energy is released and converted into kinetic energy—the energy of motion. The energy is transferred to the projectile (launched object), which then flies in the air.

CATAPULTS

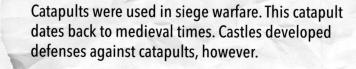

Catapults were used in siege warfare. This catapult dates back to medieval times. Castles developed defenses against catapults, however.

The first use of the catapult was in China. Later, they were used by the ancient Greeks and Romans. Alexander the Great used them as he built his empire.

A trebuchet is a type of catapult. The long arm throws the projectile. The long arm can be either controlled by people pulling ropes or activated by a counterweight.

The stones used in catapults were generally round and smooth. Specific types of stone were used to produce the greatest damage. Catapults could also be loaded with incendiary devices or debris.

PAPER

Paper was invented more than 2,000 years ago in ancient China. It is most commonly used for writing, drawing, packaging, and printing. Without paper we wouldn't have books, newspapers, magazines, or even money.

WHAT CAME BEFORE PAPER?

Before paper was created, cave drawings were used to communicate. Other methods used to reach out to others were smoke signals and drums. The ancient Egyptians made a kind of paper from the papyrus plant. Papyrus is where the word paper comes from.

HOW IS PAPER MADE?

Did you know that the paper you write on every day is generally made from trees? Paper can be made from flax, cotton, and hemp, among other plant fibers, but mostly it is made from logs or from recycled paper that itself was made from logs.

HOW IS PAPER MADE?

It all gets started with the cutting down of trees. The trees are then sent, in log form, to a paper factory, or mill. The bark must be peeled from the trees. Then the wood is chopped into very small pieces. These wood pieces are boiled with water and a few other chemicals until they turn into a slushy, mushy pulp.

The pulp is then poured through a strainer to separate the pulp from the liquid. The thick pulp is then squeezed between felt-covered press rollers to absorb extra water. This pulp mat now passes through hot rollers, as many times as necessary, until it is completely dry. Once it's fully dried, the paper is ready. It comes in roll form, much like the way you see toilet paper or paper towels at home. Paper can also be output in huge sheets.

MAKE YOUR OWN PATTERNED PAPER

You can buy pretty patterned stationery, or create your own with just water and food coloring.

MATERIALS

- Food coloring
- Squeeze or spray bottles
- Paper (absorbent, textured paper works best)
- Paper towels
- Newspaper or an old sheet

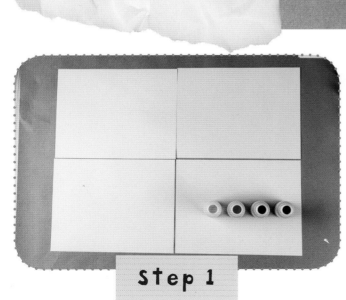

Step 1

Lay out the sheets of paper you want to decorate. This can get messy, so it's best to have them on a surface that can be cleaned easily, or to put down an old sheet or newspapers. Fill the bottles with water and a few drops of food coloring.

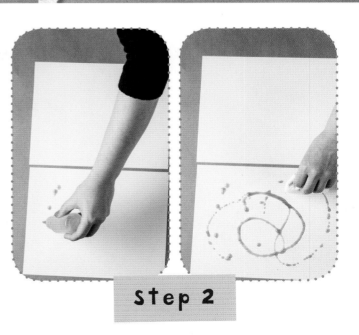

Step 2

Spray or spritz the paper with the colorful water.

Step 3

Step 4

Gently blot extra water away with a paper towel.

You can mix colors!

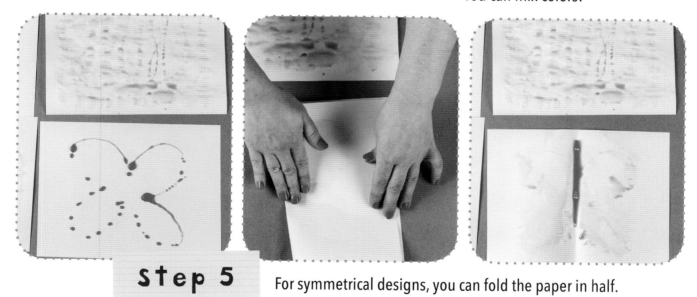

Step 5

For symmetrical designs, you can fold the paper in half.

Step 6

Leave your designs overnight to dry.

JUMPING FROG

Make a frog that jumps with just a sheet of 3" by 3" paper. Press down on the frog's back and it will hop!

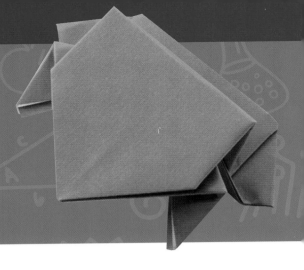

Step 1

Position your paper as a square, with the blank side facing up.

Step 2

Bring the left side of the paper over to make a rectangle.

Step 3

Bring the top left corner of the rectangle over to the right edge of the paper.

Step 4

Unfold to see the crease you just created.

Step 5

Do the same with the right corner.

Step 6

Flip the paper over. Bring the top of the paper down and create a fold. The fold should cross the intersection of your two diagonal creases.

Step 7

Then unfold to see the crease you just created and flip the paper over again.

Step 8

Touch the center point as shown in the picture, and then bring in the sides to create a triangular shape.

Step 9

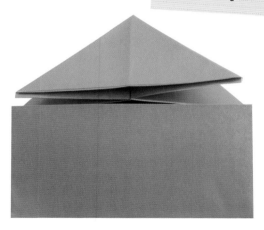

Bring up the bottom half of the model to the bottom of the triangle.

Step 10

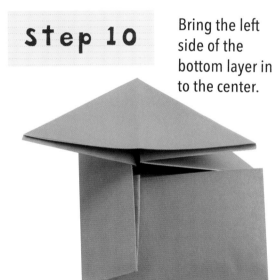

Bring the left side of the bottom layer in to the center.

Step 11

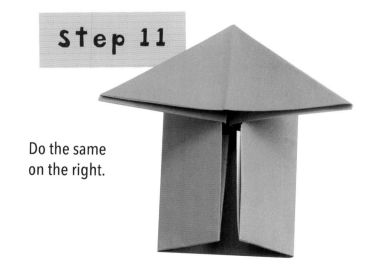

Do the same on the right.

Step 12

Fold the tip of the triangle up as shown. This creates the frog's front leg.

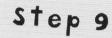

Step 13

Do the same on the other side.

Step 14

Fold the top layer of the bottom right corner of the model as shown. Do the same on the other side.

Step 15

Fold the frog in half, bringing the top layer down to the bottom corner.

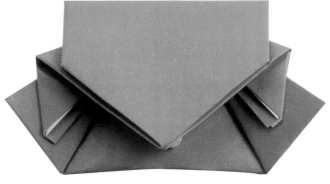
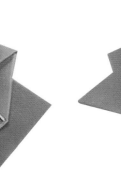

Step 16

Flip the frog over so that you're seeing the square of its back.

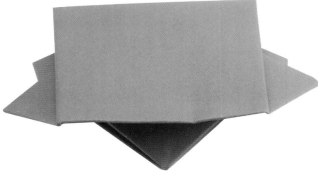

Step 17

Bring the bottom of the square back and fold it in half.

Step 18

Press down on the base of the frog's back and release to make it hop away!

ORIGAMI PINWHEEL

Step 1

Position your paper with the color/pattern facing up.

Step 2

Fold from left to right and then open the paper. Fold from the top to the bottom and open the paper.

Step 3

Create two more folds along the diagonal lines. Open the paper; you should see the fold lines as shown in the picture.

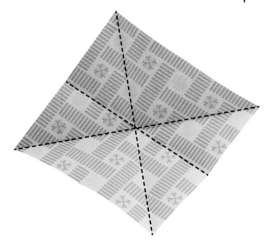

Step 4

Bring one corner of the paper in to the center of the paper.

Step 5

Do the same with the other three corners.

Step 6

Open the paper back up.

Step 7

Flip it over.

Step 8

Fold each edge to the center line, then unfold the paper.

Step 9

Do the same with the opposite edges. Then unfold the paper.

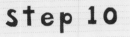

Step 10

Fold over two edges as shown, leaving the corner out.

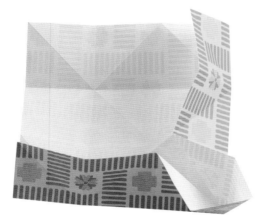

Step 11

Now flatten the corner as shown.

Step 12

Moving clockwise, do the same for the next corner.

Step 13

The last two folds will be flattened in one step.

LIGHT AND MIRRORS

Light is a form of energy—and it's the fastest thing in the universe. Light travels at a speed of 186,282 miles per second. Our main source of light energy is the Sun. Light takes about eight minutes to travel the 93 million miles from the Sun to our Earth.

VISIBLE SPECTRUM

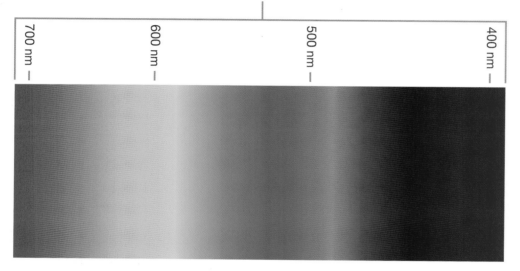

700 nm — 600 nm — 500 nm — 400 nm —

Red   Orange   Yellow   Green   Blue   Indigo   Violet

Different colors of light travel at different wavelengths. Beyond the visible spectrum are infrared and ultraviolet light. Some animals can see in those ranges.

Light travels in a straight line, but when it enters a transparent material, it can bend. This change is called refraction. The lenses of glasses, as well as microscopes and telescopes, use refraction to affect how we see.

When white light enters a prism, it breaks into its separate colors. Since each color travels at a different speed, it bends a different amount, producing a rainbow effect.

Some materials absorb light or scatter it. Others, particularly smooth, shiny surfaces, reflect back the photons that make up light.

Kaleidoscopes have mirrors inside that are angled to reflect light in a way that produces a symmetrical pattern.

KALEIDOSCOPE

Make something beautiful with colored beads and reflective paper.

MATERIALS

- Reflective wrapping paper
- Cardboard tube
- Plastic wrap
- Beads
- Construction paper
- Ruler
- Compass
- Scissors
- Tape

Step 1

Cut a piece of construction paper and wrap it around the cardboard tube.

Step 2

Cover one side of the tube with construction paper, taping it to the sides.

Step 3

Use the sharp end of the compass to poke a hole in the center of the circle.

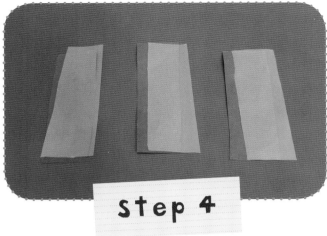

Step 4

Cut three rectangular pieces of construction paper and three matching rectangles from the reflective paper. They should be slightly shorter than the length of the tube.

Step 5

Form a pyramid, with the three pieces of reflective paper on the inside. Slide it inside the tube.

Step 6

Cover the other end of the tube with plastic wrap. Add some beads.

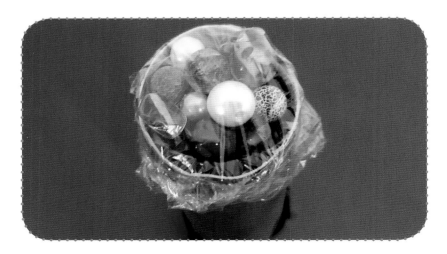

Step 7

Cover the beads with another bit of plastic wrap and tape it securely. When you look through the hole at the other end, you will see your beads and their reflections from the reflective paper, forming a beautiful pattern!

GET RICH QUICK?

See refraction in action with this simple experiment.

MATERIALS

- Glass of water
- Coin

Step 1

Drop the penny into the water. From above, you simply see the penny.

Step 2

From other angles, it looks like the glass contains two pennies! The rays of light bend as they enter the water, producing an illusion of a second coin.